Ultimate Play-Along | Dr...

VIRGIL DONATI

ISBN 0-7390-3895-8 (Book & 2 CDs)

Ultimate Play-Along | DrumTrax
VIRGIL DONATI

Transcriptions: **Virgil Donati, Rick Gratton, Bruno Meeus, Tim Davies**
Music Engraving: **Rick Gratton**
Photography: **Alex Solca, Dean Freeze, Yasuhiko Roppongi**
Musicians: **Phil Turcio, Simon Hosford, Evripides Evripidou, Ricc Fierabracci,**
Derek Sherinian, Tony MacAlpine, T. J. Helmerich, Brett Garsed, Tom Kennedy
Audio Engineers: **Tom Fletcher, T. J. Helmerich**
Assistants: **Rob Brill, Scott Francisco, Roy Burns**
Audio CD Loops Editing: **Rick Gratton and Jack Preobrazenski, Preomusic Productions Inc.**
Content Editing: **Rick Gratton, Ray Brych**
Book Design and Layout: **Rick Gratton and Ed Uribe for Dancing Planet MediaWorks**

Contents

Drum Loops

Acknowledgements

This book archives the ideas of some of my most progressive recorded performances, and could not have been realized without the invaluable talents and contributions of the following people: Rick Gratton, Bruno Meeus, Tim Davies; to all the musicians—Phil, Simon, Evri, Ricc, Derek, T Mac, T. J. Brett, and Tom—my thanks for your legendary performances and to David Hakim, Ray Brych, and Mike Finkelstien for making this a reality.

Warming up backstage in Tilburg, Holland.

Virgil arrested in Louisiana for excessive noise while soundchecking for a clinic.

About the Author

"After all these years of playing, I still feel like I've barely scratched the surface!"

—*Virgil Donati*

"Many drummers come to mind who've had a hand in raising the bar—leading by example with faster chops, innovative use of the instrument, more complex rhythms, more creative phrasing, and, in general, inspiring a new generation of drummers. But few have turned as many heads as Virgil Donati."

—*Stick It Magazine, Feb. 1998*

Virgil was born and raised in Melbourne, Australia. From the time he could barely utter a word, he keenly observed the regular band rehearsals his father held in the house. Virgil's interest in music and instinct for rhythm had been apparent to his parents for some time. They began considering a musical path for him, and one month prior to turning three, he found himself sitting behind his first real drumset.

Within months, he was already on stage, performing guest spots with his fathers show band. At six years of age, Virgil also started piano lessons, which cultivated the skills he would later call upon for composing music. The gigs with his father continued until 12 years of age, when he began working with other local bands.

Joining his first rock band and signing with his first major label at age 15 was surely the right choice for the young drummer. The band was called "Cloud Nine," later to become "Taste." This was to give Virgil his early experiences in the studio, with three releases by the band. The relentless touring also allowed him to cultivate and improve his skills on stage.

At the age of 16, Virgil turned pro, enabling him to tour and focus on music, and has since devoted his whole life and soul to his art. The motivation has been his endless and restless pursuit to express himself through his playing.

At age 19, Virgil traveled to the U.S. to further study drumming, and also took classes in composition and arranging. One of the highlights of his drum studies, was the opportunity to have lessons with jazz legend Philly Joe Jones.

Returning to Australia at age 21, his career was alight. He was in demand, playing many genres of music, including jazz, rock, pop, theater and studio work. He also worked with many visiting artists, including jazz pianist George Cables, vocalist Mark Murphy, Branford Marsalis, Kenny Kirkland, and Melissa Etheridge.

His next taste of commercial success came in the early '90s with Southern Sons. The band reached double platinum with their debut album. At the same time, throughout the mid '80s and '90s, Virgil's interest in progressive music found a voice with several bands he initiated, most notably Loose Change, and later, On the Virg.

In 1996, Virgil uprooted and relocated in the U.S.A. in an attempt to expand onto the world stage. It has since proved to be a very rewarding and productive time. Recording and touring with the likes of Planet X, Steve Vai, Steve Walsh, Derek Sherinian, Scott Henderson, Tribal Tech, Cab, Bunny Brunel, Frank Gambale, Tony MacAlpine, Joel Hoekstra, Ricc Fierabracci, Mark Boals, Dave Stewart, Mick Jagger, and many others, he continues to push the limits of the instrument to astonishing new levels.

Discography

Bunny Brunel
L.A. Zoo Revisited (2003, Brunel Music)

Derek Sherinian
Planet X (1999, Magna Carta)

Erik Norlander
Music Machine (2003, Avalon/Think Tank/Transmission)

Freakhouse
Beautiful Misery (2003, Sony/Reality Entertainment)

Garsed & Helmerich
Under the Lash of Gravity (1999, Cooee Music)

Jesus Christ Superstar
1992 Australian Cast Recording (1992, Emerald City)

Joel Hoekstra
Undefined (2000, Sony)
The Moon Is Falling (2003, Joel Hoekstra)

Jon Stevens
Are You Satisfied? (1993)
Circles (1996, Sony)

Loose Change
Live at the Grainstore (2004, Vorticity)

Mark Boals
Ring of Fire (2001, Avalon/Marquee)

On The Virg
Serious Young Insects (1999, Vorticity)

Planet X
Universe (2000, Century Media)
Live From Oz (2002, Inside Out Music)
Moon Babies (2002, Inside Out Music)

Ring of Fire
Burning Live In Tokyo (2002, Avalon/Marquee)
Oracle (2002, Avalon/Marquee)
Ring of Fire (2003, Frontiers)
Lapse of Reality (2004, Avalon)

Southern Sons
Southern Sons (1990, BMG/RCA)
Nothing But The Truth (1992, BMG/Arista)
Zone (1996, BMG/RCA)

The State
Elementary (1998, BMG/Arista)

Steve Walsh
Glossolalia (2000, Magna Carta)

Virgil Donati
Stretch (1995, Musos Publications)
Just Add Water (1997, Musos Publications)

Introduction

To follow a creative pursuit is to have the greatest purpose in existence. Creativity gives you individual freedom. It breaks the shackles of conditioning, and provides an opportunity to search out your own way. I always felt the need to discover, understand and expand the rhythmic and tonal possibilities of my instrument; to craft an individual sound that goes beyond what the text books can give you. I have always accepted the nature of the instrument to be physically and mentally challenging. Night after night, performance after performance, extending your endurance and expanding your creativity; reaching beyond all limits. The vitality and excitement in the controlled pounding of hypnotic rhythms or explosive polyrhythmic structures. The ability to create a musical, visual and emotional experience for an audience. This is the heart of drumming.

Though our initial training is directed at overcoming the technical hurdles, it must never be forgotten that music is much more than this. It is the development of our imagination that really enables us to broaden what is possible on the instrument. This is how we develop true expressive meaning in our playing. Music is so much more than just technical development. It is an art form that expresses our highest aspirations, ideals, passions and beliefs. This is the soul of drumming.

How far one travels on such an adventure is dependent on personal commitment, desire, and musical taste. Today our musical culture is incredibly rich and diverse. What was once considered to be absolutely correct in popular music, is no longer necessarily the case. Our culture no longer provides us with all the rules as to what is ultimately right or wrong. Awareness of this diversity gives us the greatest freedom of all. The character and expressive nature of your performance becomes just as important as your technical adequacy. This is the new culture of drumming.

If you keep a humble perspective, and you do the very best you can, then ultimately what you are supposed to do here on this earth will come to you. You may not always get everything that you desire, but you will get enough of what you need to keep going. This is the nature of drumming.

Notation Key

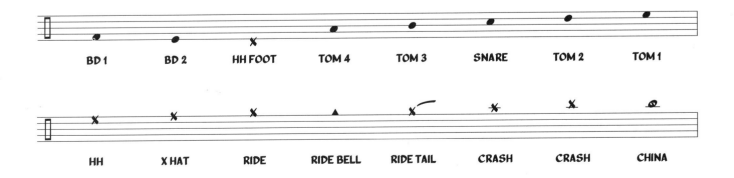

T. J., Virgil, Ricc, and Brett.

Simon Hosford.

Phil Turcio.

Ricc Fierabracci.

On The Virg backstage.

Pyramids on Mars

Virgil's Thoughts

This piece from the *On The Virg* CD, starts with a deceptive bass drum part. There is no initial reference to the true meter, so our perception is that the bass drum is simply playing quarter notes. Several bars later, when the hi-hat and snare parts are introduced, a more complex layered rhythm begins to reveal itself. It becomes apparent that perhaps what we thought were quarter notes may be something else altogether. You may start to perceive some different possibilities. The time signature is actually $\frac{7}{16}$, and the bass drum is playing every third sixteenth note, starting on the downbeat of the first bar:

It loops itself in a three bar cycle, and can also be thought of as 7 against 3, if you view the groups of seven as septuplets rather than bars of $\frac{7}{16}$:

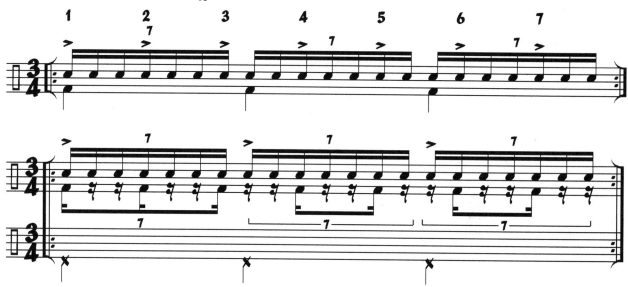

The rhythm becomes a little more elaborate as we add the hands. Firstly, the hi-hat plays eighth notes in $\frac{7}{16}$ time. This can also be thought of as every second sixteenth note, starting on the downbeat of the first bar and on the upbeat of the second bar, creating an over-the-bar-line effect. I also add an accent on every second hi-hat beat, which gives the feeling of being in 4:

The snare drum is playing strong backbeats on the first beat of bars 2 and 3. However, there are also some subtle ghost notes, which add a nice flow to the groove:

The sixteenth notes are moving at a fast pace and I recommend practicing at a slow tempo at first to learn how to count and eventually feel these odd groupings.

At the end of the $\frac{7}{16}$ section, the piece opens up into a steady $\frac{4}{4}$ groove (B section). From here, we are led to a half time C section, which is very sparse. We have traveled from a complex layered opening section and gradually arrived to this very open exposed section.

All these elements have been placed into some kind of cohesive form.

As we set up this solo section, we enter into a $\frac{6}{4}$ groove which ends with a fill at bar 117 to set up the solo. Analyzing this fill, we discover a mix of quintuplets and sixteenth-note triplets that creates a perfect setup for the solo section.

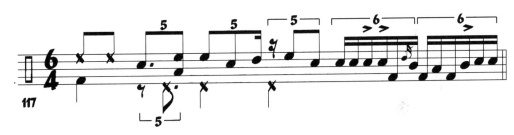

At the end of the solo we return to the A section. Here, I play a variation of the original feel. The left foot plays a polyrhythmic figure on the bass drum. It is playing 2 against the 7 feel.

This example shows how to accurately place the 2 against 7:

When we put it all together, we get this:

As we crescendo towards the ending, we make a subtle transition from the $\frac{7}{16}$ feel to $\frac{6}{4}$.

Virgil, Brett, and T.J.

Pyramids on Mars (Drum Transcription)

Virgil Donati

Pyramids on Mars

Pyramids on Mars 5-5

Virgil soundchecking in Tokyo.

OTV Live.

Native Metal

Virgil's Thoughts

The introduction of this tune from the *On The Virg* CD, features a very processed guitar sound which is setting up the riff in letter A. The meter is four bars of $\frac{7}{16}$ followed by two bars of $\frac{4}{4}$. The drums enter with unison singles between the hands and feet. I like the powerful effect of this unison figure. Note also the flam on the downbeats of each bar. The groove starting at letter A alternates between four bars of $\frac{7}{16}$ and two bars of $\frac{4}{4}$.

Letter B starts with three bars of $\frac{4}{4}$ followed by a $\frac{5}{16}$ section that could also be thought of in $\frac{5}{4}$:

Let's break it down further. The first five beats of the above example are re-written as $\frac{5}{16}$. With the two time signatures played back to back, you can analyze each measure in a similar manner for easy execution.

I prefer to think of it in $\frac{5}{16}$ mainly because that's what I heard when composing it, and it does have an overall effect on how I phrase this section.

Although letter C, starting at bar 95, can give the impression that it's in 5, it is in $\frac{4}{4}$ as dictated by the snare backbeats. It is the bass drum pattern that is phrased over the bar line in $\frac{5}{4}$. Again, it's possible to interpret and think of it either way. I concede that going with the guitar phrasing is the easier alternative, and I tend to do this when playing it live.

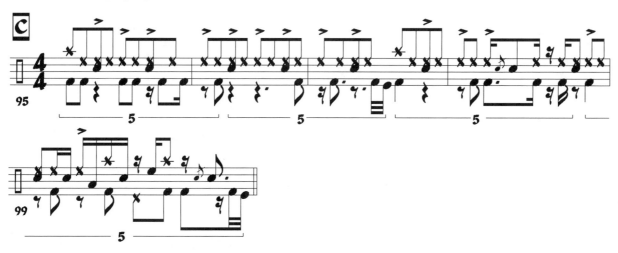

Letter D is an example of rhythm bending. To some, it may sound as if the tempo is changing but in fact, it remains strong and steady; it's the change of rhythmic phrasing that has this effect. It changes from sixteenth notes to sixteenth-note triplets back to sixteenth notes and then finally to eighth-note triplets. Presented is the D section taken from the play-along chart that will help simplify these rhythmic phrasings.

Presented is a simplified version of the groove in the first part of the solo section at letter E, starting on bar 116. Note that the hi-hat pattern is the same as the $\frac{7}{16}$ hi-hat pattern in the "Pyramids" example. The kick plays beat 1 of every bar and the snare plays on beat 5 in the first three bars and beat 4 in the fourth bar.

It's interesting to note the different ways the ear can interpret certain rhythms. This tune is a good example of how we can play the same pattern and yet have it feel totally different by thinking of it in these alternate time signatures.

Virgil Donati

Native Metal

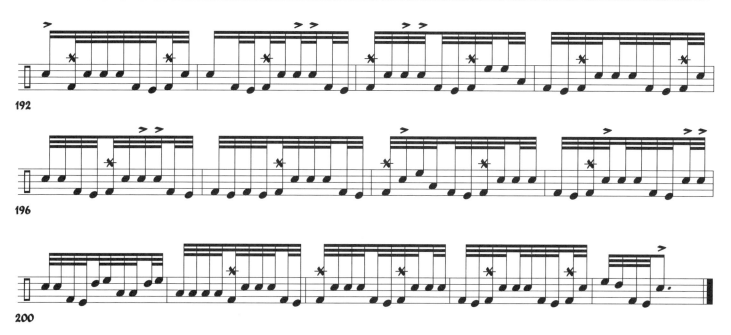

192

196

200

Native Metal 6-6

Cutting the OTV tracks.

At Oasis Mastering with Gene Grimaldi mastering the OTV record.

Technical problems at the OTV session.

Choosing drums for the OTV session.

Invasion
of the Ants

Virgil's Thoughts

During the acoustic guitar intro of this tune off of the *On The Virg* CD, the drums are tacet with the exception of a few cymbal swells. The snare fill introduces the meter and this $\frac{3}{4}$ feel continues throughout the A section. The melody enters on the B section, as does a meter change to $\frac{4}{4}$. I play a steady rock groove throughout the B section with some fills at the end of phrases.

The C section starts to open up a little. The hi-hat is splashier than the previous section and then I move to the ride half-way through the section. Four bars further on, I double the snare feel and build to a final crash on bar 52.

We return to the intro 3/4 groove for the keyboard solo at letter D.

The first eight bars are quite intense and we then drop the dynamic drastically for the start of the solo. Again, as with the previous section, we start to build the level of intensity along with the soloist. This time, it is far more gradual, being an extended solo. I start to reach a peak when I go to the ride and bring in the single stroke pattern on the kick drum. For the very last eight bars of the solo, starting at bar 111, the kick drum pattern changes from 16th notes to 32nd notes with the snare playing on all downbeats.

This is one of the challenges of double bass drumming—playing a fast single stroke pattern with the feet without sacrificing quality. This eight-bar pattern is also a great speed building exercise. Try to maintain accuracy and volume.

We drop down to acoustic guitar again at bar 119, and then go back to the melody until the outro hits at the end, bar 139, where we ad lib fills until the last hit. On the track minus the drums, you'll here the click track keeping you in time between the hits. This is how I recorded it. When you remove the click, you are under the impression that it's all played on cue and out of time but in fact it was all done to a click, just as you hear it. When playing this part live, the hits would be played rubato on my cue.

Invasion of the Ants (Drum Transcription)

Invasion of the Ants 5-1

Invasion of the Ants 5-2

Invasion of the Ants

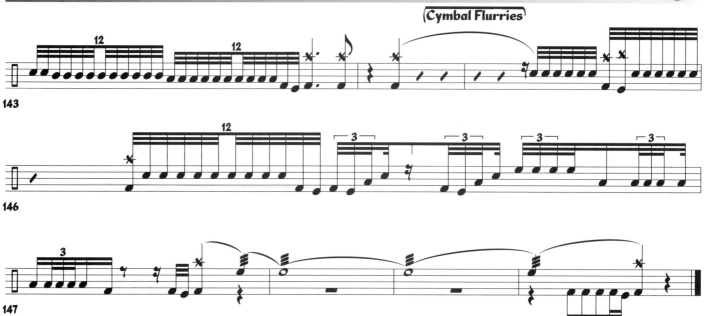

143

146

147

Invasion of the Ants 5-5

John Tempesta and Virgil.

Steve Gadd and Virgil.

Alien
Hip Hop

Virgil's Thoughts

The opening fill of this track from the *On The Virg* CD, is a composite of eighth- and sixteenth-note triplets. This leads us into the main theme of this piece, which is the groove in the A section. On first listening, it gives the impression of being in an odd time signature, but if you focus on the snare playing the heavy backbeats on 2 and 4, you'll soon realize that, in fact, it's all in $\frac{4}{4}$. It is the bass drum pattern playing across the bar line that can be deceiving. If you carefully analyze this bass drum pattern, you will notice that it loops itself every 16 beats. As a result, it takes four measures for the pattern to resolve itself. Note: included is a single bass drum version of this piece in the play-along section.

Here it is in $\frac{16}{8}$.

Adding the snare and hi-hat overtop, we get this:

This was the groove I originally composed and then transposed into $\frac{4}{4}$ time to arrive at the final version. When the snare starts to catch the keyboard hits at bar 21, you'll notice that the hits are related to the above $\frac{16}{8}$ example.

Another possibility, although extremely challenging, is to play the bass drum pattern as an ostinato while soloing with the hands. I now do this as part of the live arrangement when I return to the A section later in the tune. The B and C sections are steady rock grooves. When playing along with the track minus drums, concentrate on the click and lock in as much as possible.

There are two interesting riffs towards the end which need special attention.

Beginning at letter D, bar 141, we play another broken triplet pattern with the feet while maintaining a steady backbeat with the snare. This figure is played in unison with the bass and guitar, and repeats six times. On the fifth and sixth time, starting at bar 149, we catch the keyboard hits with the snare. Notice that these snare hits all fall where the rests occur in the bass drum part and take note of the economical sticking patterns played on the third and fourth bars of each pass between the hi-hat and snare.

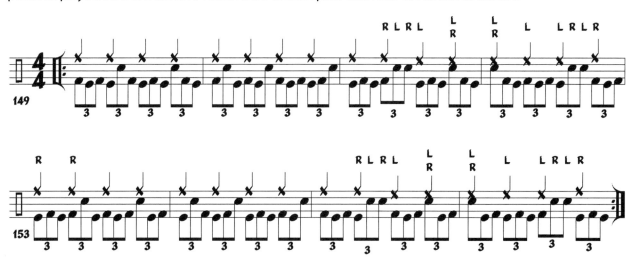

At letter E, we launch a heavy single stroke triplet groove with the feet only interrupting the eighth note triplets by occasionally inserting a sixteenth-note triplet. The riff is a five measure repeat. On the third repeat I move to a China cymbal with the right hand. On the fourth repeat, I change from playing quarter-notes to quarter-note triplets on the China and on the final repeat the snare plays every fourth quarter note triplet in unison with the China. This has the character of a "metric modulation," but it is rather just a rhythmic modulation.

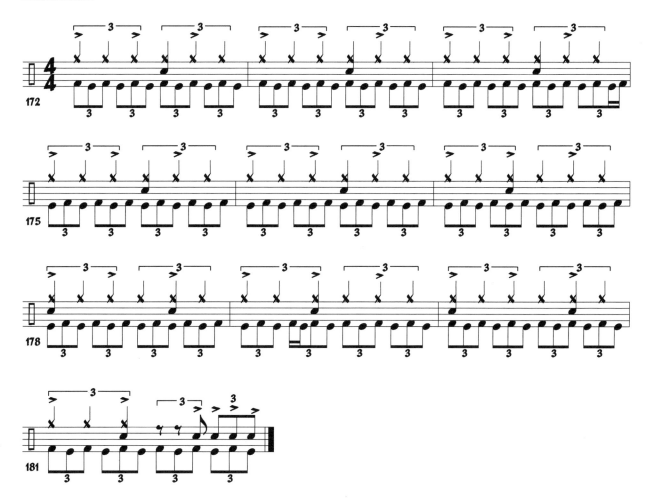

Alien Hip Hop (Transcription)

Virgil Donati

Alien Hip Hop

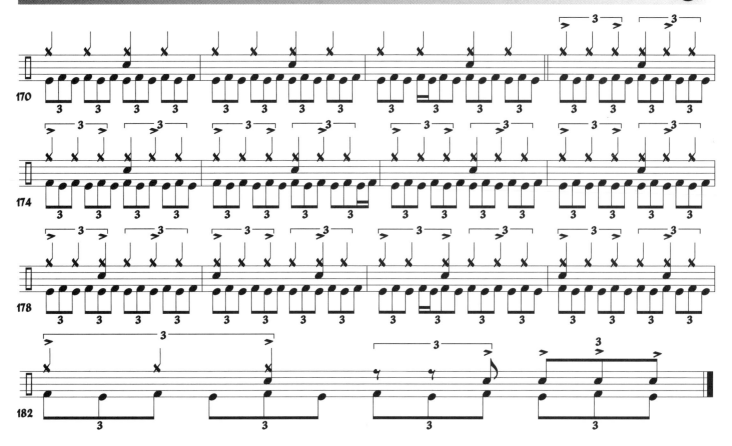

Alien Hip Hop 5-5

Virgil with Alan and Ron Vater turning Virgil's Assault sticks.

Dog Boots

Virgil's Thoughts

The main component of this track played on the *Universe* CD is the relentless double kick groove. It is played as inverted double stroke rolls. For me, this was an invaluable technique to master, being the only possible way I could have sustained this tempo for the 3:17 minute duration of the piece.

Here is a breakdown of the inverted double strokes with each limb isolated :

Right Bass Drum

Left Bass Drum

Here are a few double bass drum variations of double strokes for you to practice. Endurance is a key factor when learning to apply these double bass drum patterns in a tune like "Dog Boots." Progressive repetition is a key factor. Tempos should strive on a daily basis to reach the desired goal with consistent practice and patience.

A

B

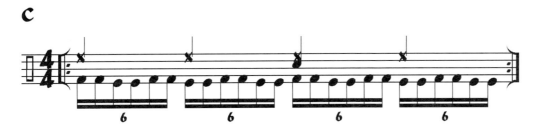

Most of the piece is self-evident, given the hypnotic, unrelenting nature of the bass drum part. The E (chorus) section, starting on bar 41 of this piece, is probably the most challenging and requires some special attention. While maintaining the groove with the kick and snare, the ride cymbal plays the ensemble phrase which is in $\frac{7}{4}$. Here is the cymbal pattern minus kick and snare:

This is what the cymbal pattern looks like without the underlying groove in $\frac{4}{4}$:

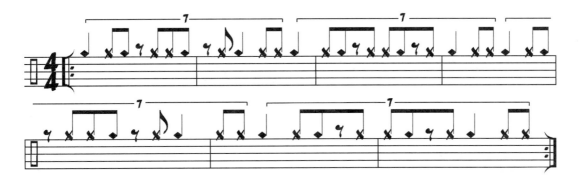

Let's add a simple kick and snare back beat to the basic ride pattern to incorporate them as a warm up exercise. Once mastered, applying the original double bass drum pattern will make more sense and be easier to execute.

The second half of the tune is basically the same form with the main difference being the double chorus at the very end.

Dog Boots (Drum Transcription)

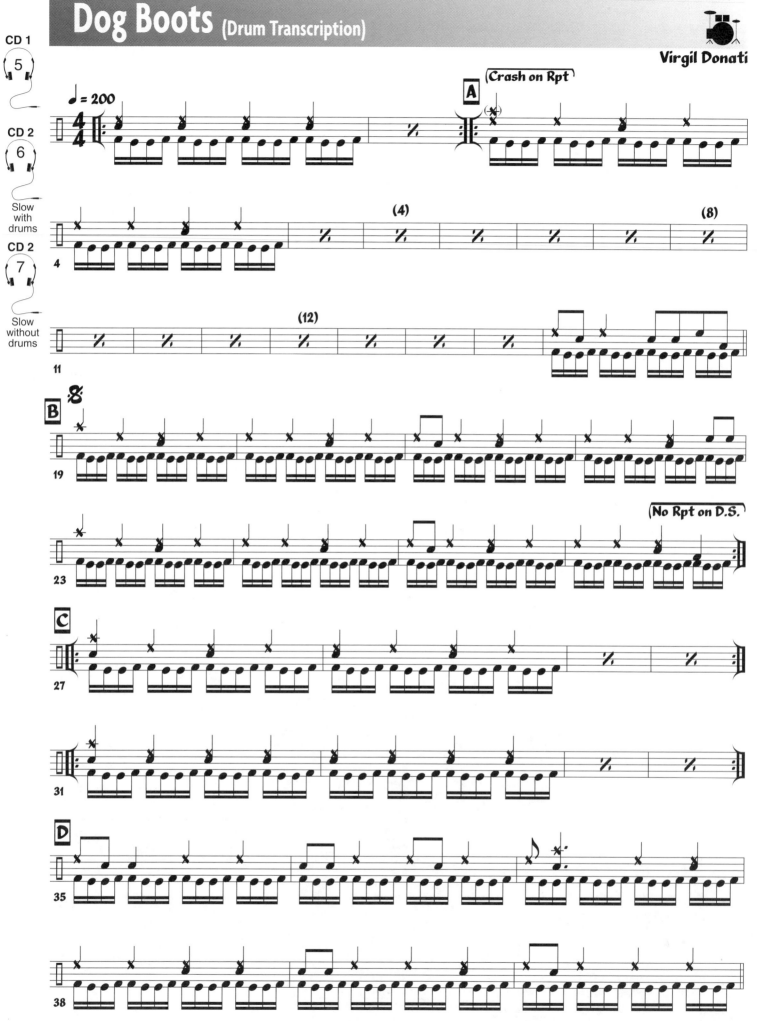

Dog Boots 5-1

Dog Boots

D.S. al Coda

✠ **Coda**

Bitch

Virgil's Thoughts

I completed writing this track towards the end of 1999 when I was about to leave for Australia to tour with OTV. We played it on that tour but as it turned out, Derek Sherinian talked me into using it for the *Universe* record.

It starts out with a heavy driving rock groove in the A section. Make sure you really focus on the click and lock in with your groove. In the B section, starting at bar 17, we have some phrasing issues to think about, particularly on the fourth and second beats of bars 18 and 19. You might want to isolate these bars and play it slowly until you master the pattern.

The A and B sections repeat, then we arrive at the chorus (C section). As with all these charts, don't be too concerned with following all of my drum parts/fills. Just listen and focus in on the other instruments and the click track. That will be your guide.

For example, this is the keyboard and bass part for the chorus. I've included this chart so you can see the phrasing and help you decide what to play to it.

The D section is in $\frac{7}{4}$ I'm playing in $\frac{4}{4}$ across it which creates an interesting rhythmical tension. Listening to the guitar will help solidify the $\frac{7}{4}$ time signature.

The ending of the piece is quite drawn out and rather dense and rich in rhythms and syncopation. Again, I thought it would serve you to follow the keyboard chart so you can clearly see the phrasing without all the drum embellishments in the drum chart.

Bitch

Virgil Donati

Bitch

Bitch

Bitch

Bitch 4-4

Greg Allen, Virgil, and Mike Farriss

Carmine Appice, Virgil, and Eric Singer.

Virgil with Scott Henderson.

Inside Black

Virgil's Thoughts

The A and B sections of this piece from the *Universe* CD are in $\frac{5}{4}$ and $\frac{7}{8}$ respectively. These two sections could be considered as the head of the tune. The long, soaring legato notes of the melody take the focus away from the underlying odd time structure, giving the listener a sense of $\frac{4}{4}$. I felt it would be important to reflect this feeling with the drum part. I achieved this by superimposing backbeats in $\frac{4}{4}$ on the snare while catching the bass/guitar riff with the bass drum. I do this in both the $\frac{5}{4}$ and the $\frac{7}{8}$ sections. If the snare were to phrase in $\frac{5}{4}$ and $\frac{7}{8}$, it would not achieve a seamless flow throughout the melody and would have an interrupted feel. You can try some different grooves when playing along with the track without drums to experience the effect your groove can have on the feel of this section.

The C section is in $\frac{4}{4}$ and is simply a bridge section leading us back to the repeat of A and B.

D is the pre-chorus leading into E, the chorus. These two sections open up into a strong $\frac{4}{4}$ rock groove. Just make it big and heavy!

F is an interlude that features some keyboard, guitar and drum unison lines, which ultimately leads us to the guitar solo. You will notice that towards the end of the unison, we play two groups of quintuplets, one of sixteenths and two of triplets, starting on bar 63 of letter G.

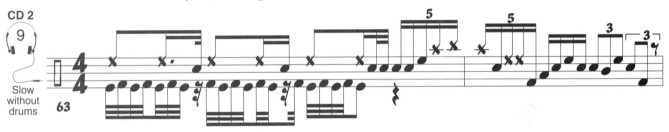

It is good practice to work on making the transition from one grouping to another until you can feel it and execute it smoothly.

The following exercises may be helpful to learn how to make these transitions accurately:

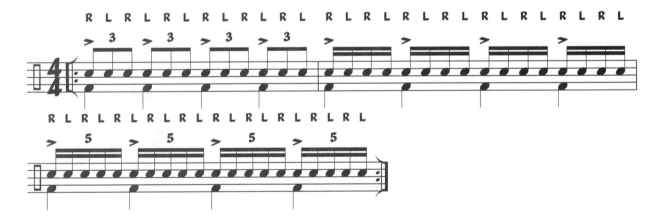

This is the sequence as it is in the piece:

The correct phrasing in 4/4 looks like this:

The coda needs some special attention. Here is a transcription of the keyboard/bass part to help clarify the phrasing starting at bar 107, leading into the coda at bar 109. After studying this chart, you can then follow the drum transcription to see how I phrased around it.

Inside Black (Drum Transcription)

Virgil Donati

Inside Black 4-1

Inside Black 4-2

Inside Black

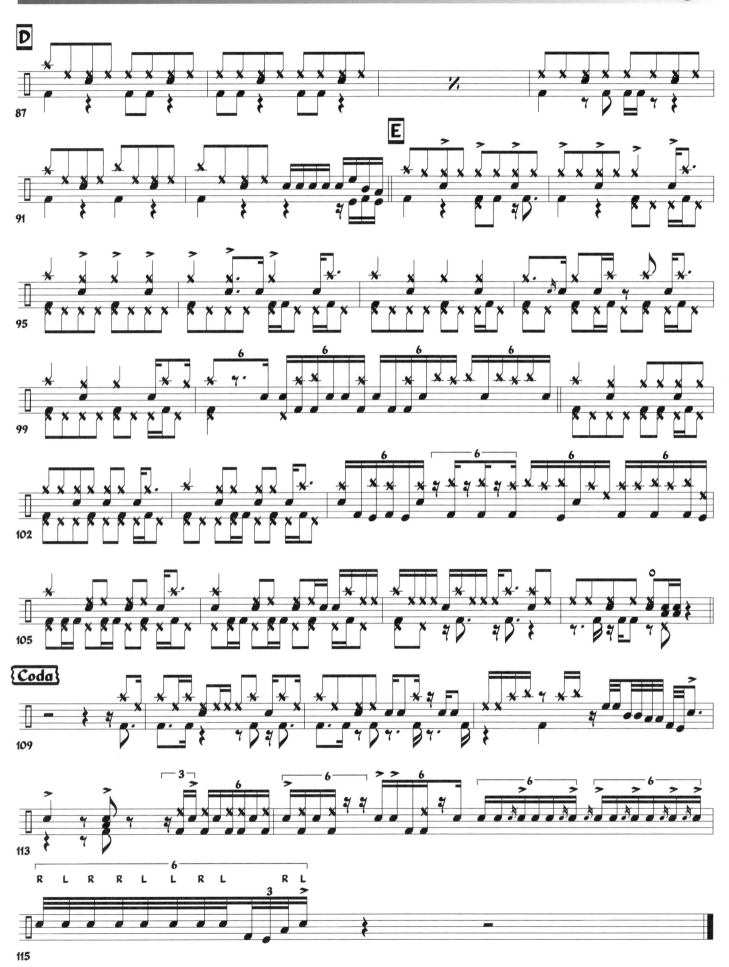

Inside Black 4-4

Planet X.

Planet X on tour in Holland.

Europa

Virgil's Thoughts

For the A and B sections of this tune off of the *Universe* CD, the approach I took was simply to play a steady backbeat while following the riff with the bass drum. I found that, over time, while playing these sections of the piece live, my ideas expanded and I started being a little more adventurous. You also may want to experiment with different possibilities when playing along with the CD.

My favorite part is the pattern at C. Notice that the meter is now $\frac{6}{4}$. I think of the bass drum pattern as three groups of four and three groups of two with a sixteenth note rest in between each group. The snare and hi-hat play straight time over this double bass drum pattern:

In the 2nd ending bar, which is the last time we play this pattern before returning to the A section, the snare replaces the rests in between the bass drum pattern. This strongly reinforces the ensemble parts just prior to the transition back to letter A.

In the D section, it is important to keep in mind the $\frac{4}{4}$ meter while trying to catch the syncopated hits along with the bass. It is good practice to count through this section and to learn which part of the beat each hit falls on. Start by just playing time and catching the hits with the bass drum. Eventually you will learn to feel it. As you gain more control, you can try to set them up with fills. This is the phrasing of the hits:

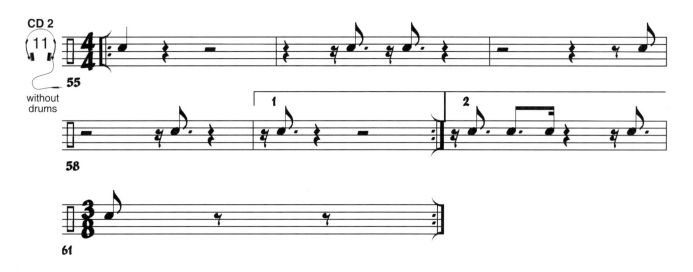

Following the keyboard solo, we have the F section in $\frac{4}{4}$ with the keyboards layering a figure in 5 over the top of it. I loosely catch some of the keyboard figures with the kick drum. This section climaxes with the ensemble catching a series of hits together. These are a slight variation of the 5's the keyboard was playing.

Note: The play-along chart and audio track minus drums for "Europa" is the live arrangement with the tempo slowed down to 130 bpm and the A section (the first verse) repeated four times and not three times as in the original recording.

Europa (Drum Transcription)

Virgil Donati

Europa - Virgil Donati/Derek Sherinian/Tony MacAlpine
© 2000 Gildon Music (BMI)/Derek Sherinian Music (BMI)/Eyes On The Prize Music (BMI)

Europa

Europa 4-4

Play-Along Charts

Pyramids on Mars (Drum Chart)

Virgil Donati

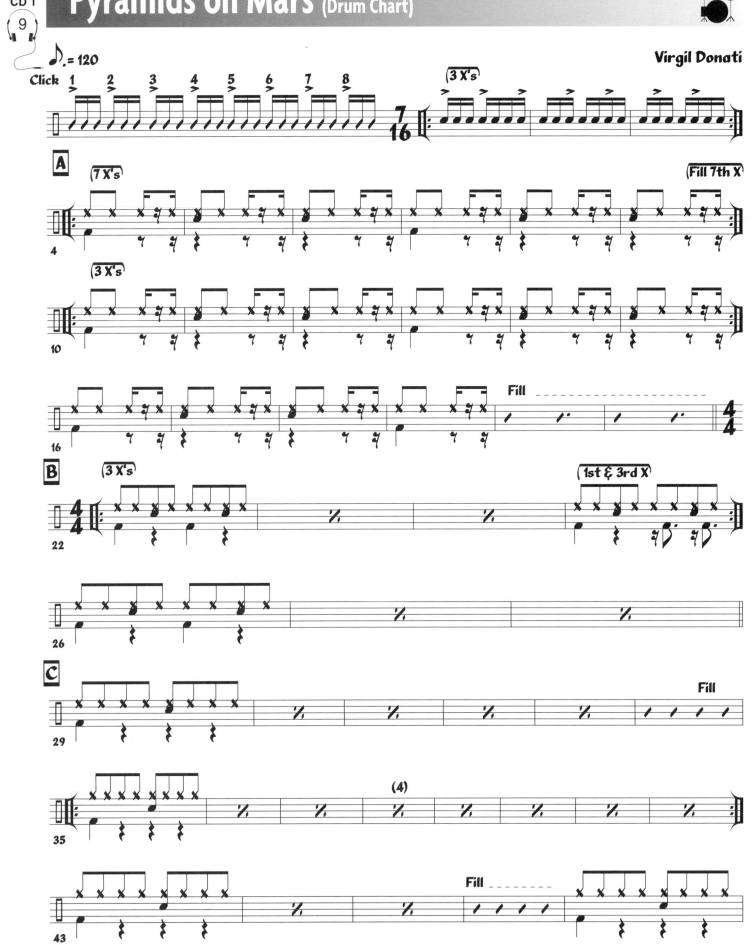

Pyramids on Mars 2-1

Native Metal (Drum Chart)

Virgil Donati

Native Metal - by Virgil Donati/Phil Turcio
© 1999 Gildon Music (BMI)/Phil Turcio (control) (APRA)
All Rights Reserved   Used by Permission

Invasion of the Ants (Drum Chart)

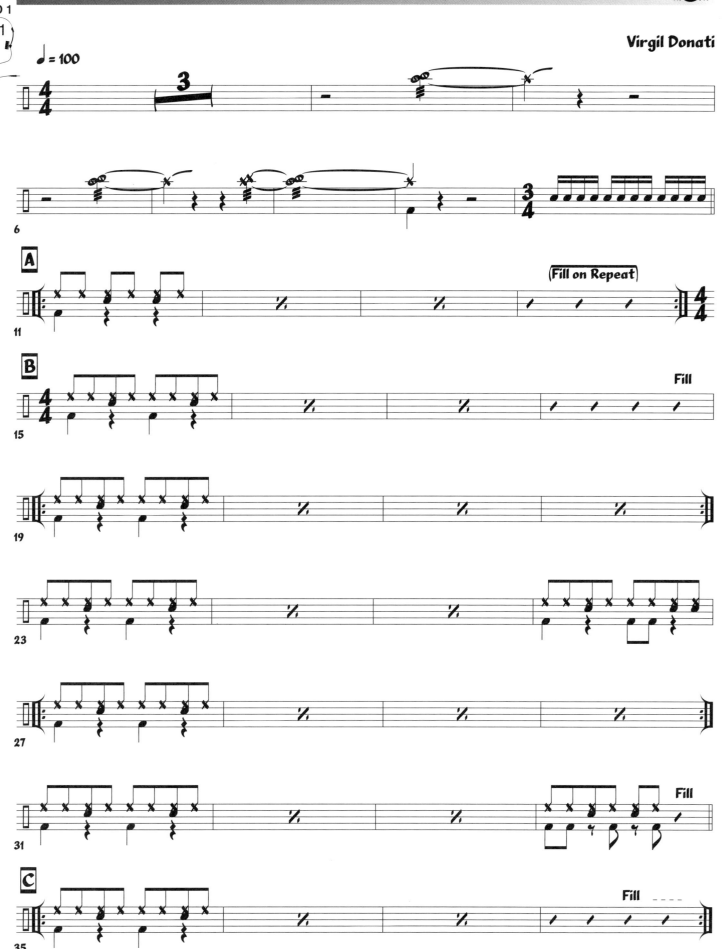

Invasion of the Ants - by Virgil Donati/T.J. Helmerich
© 1999 Gildon Music (BMI) and T.J. Helmerich Publishing Designee
All Rights Reserved   Used by Permission

Invasion of the Ants 3-1

Invasion of the Ants 3-2

Invasion of the Ants

Invasion of the Ants 3-3

Alien Hip Hop (Drum Chart 1)

CD 1

Virgil Donati

E

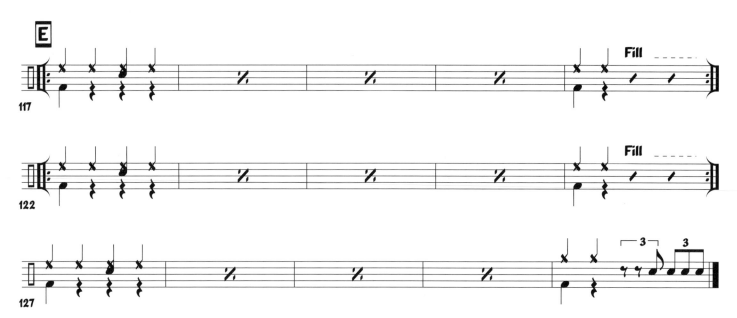

Alien Hip Hop v.1 3-1

On tour in London.

Virgil's mom.

Alien Hip Hop (Drum Chart 2)

Virgil Donati

Alien Hip Hop - by Virgil Donati

Alien Hip Hop v.2 4-2

Alien Hip Hop v.2 4-3

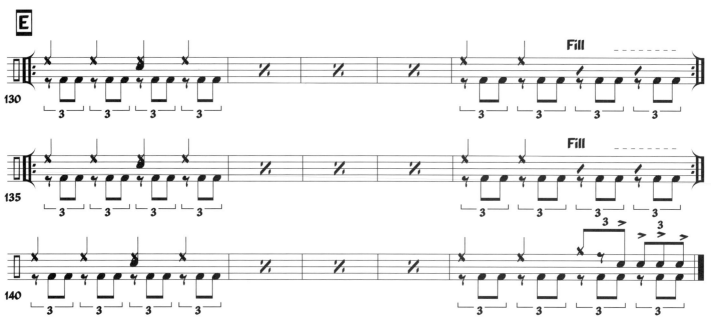

Alien Hip Hop v.2 4-4

Dog Boots (Drum Chart)

Virgil Donati

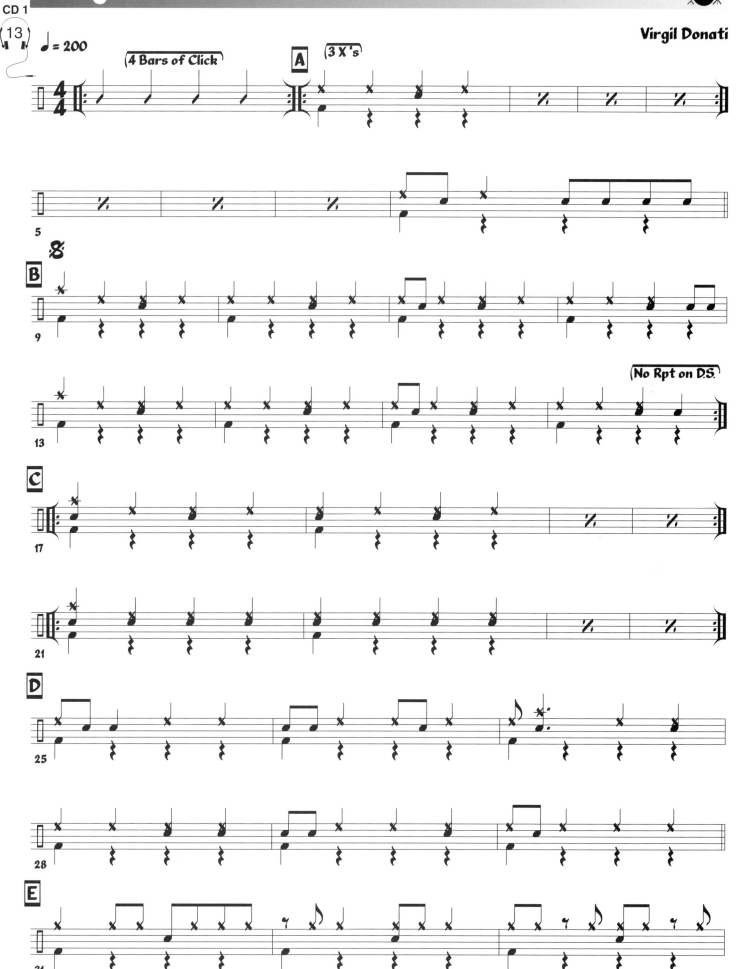

Dog Boots - by Virgil Donati
© 2000 Gildon Music (BMI)
All Rights Reserved   Used by Permission

To Coda

Dog Boots

D.S. al Coda

Coda

Dog Boots 3-3

CD 1

Virgil Donati

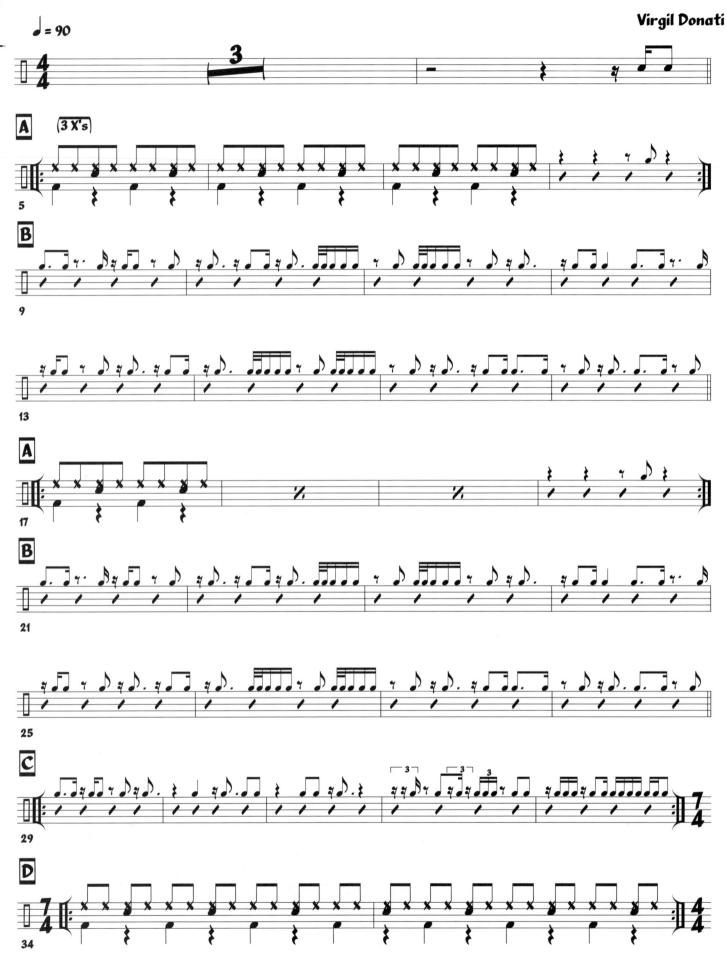

Bitch 3-1

Bitch - by Virgil Donati
© 2000 Gildon Music (BMI)

Bitch

Coda

70

73

Fill & Fade Out

77

Bitch 3-3

Inside Black (Drum Chart)

Virgil Donati

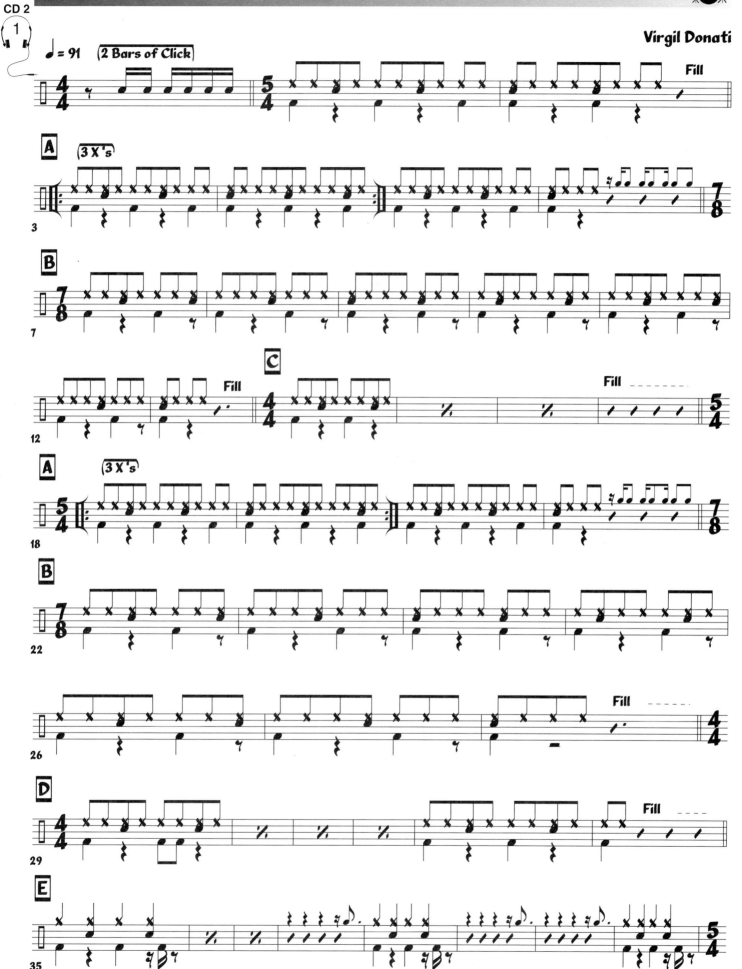

Inside Black 3-1

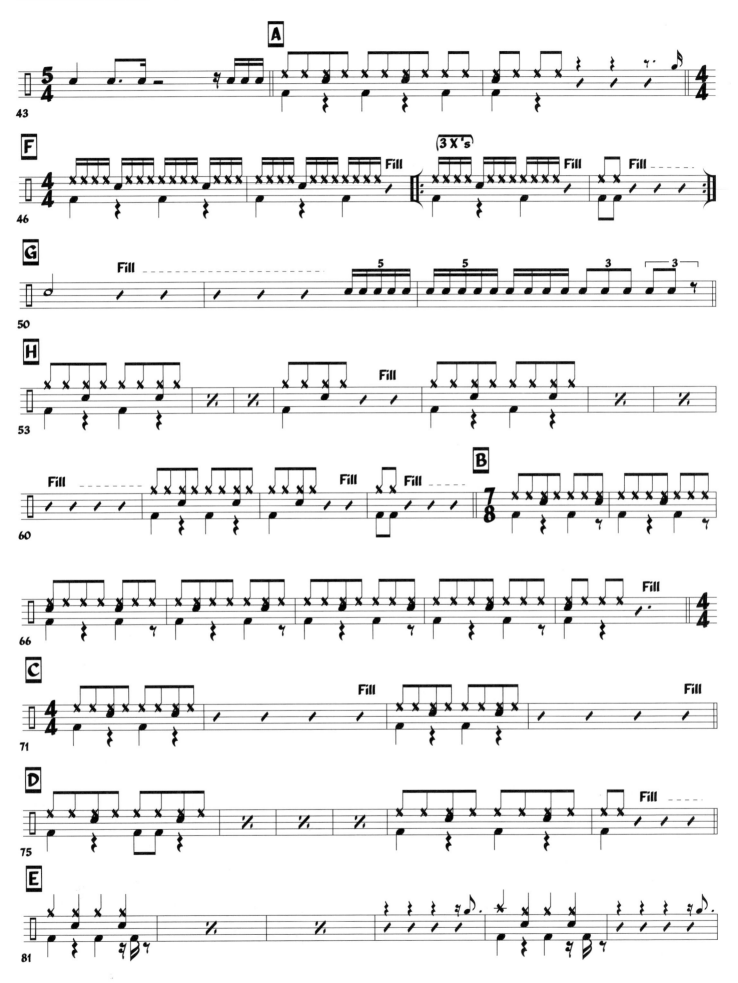

Inside Black

Inside Black 3-3

Europa (Drum Chart)

Virgil Donati

Europa 2-1

Europa

Updated News, Lessons & Highlights
Available Only on Virgil's Website!

www.virgildonati.com

VISIT VIRGIL DONATI'S
OFFICIAL WEBSITE TODAY!